Metal Detecting

Treasure Hunting Bible for Beginners

Contents

Introduction

The first metal detectors appeared in the 19th century and as a result of rapid technological developments and portability they quickly became accessible to the public towards the end of the 20th century. Ever since then, people all around the world have started metal detecting both professionally and as a hobby. Hundreds of thousands of metal detecting enthusiasts or "metal detectorists" have taken up this fun and potentially lucrative hobby for a number of reasons which include:

- Finding hidden treasures (gold, silver, historical relics, coins, etc.) that they can sell later on,
- The adrenaline rush of finding something that's been hidden for hundreds or even thousands of years and possibly has great historical or cultural significance,

- The love of collecting modern or ancient coins, jewelry, buttons, buckles, war relics and even arrowheads,

- And finally, the opportunity to get some exercise and be outdoors (fields, parks, beaches, woodlands, etc.) which is an added bonus for many metal detectorists.

Regardless of your reasons to try metal detecting, it's very important to know how to go about it. Many people have dived into metal detecting without taking the time to find out the techniques and strategies of searching, the subtleties of searching different locations, the different types of metal detectors out there (and which one is best for you), how to research a location before searching it, as well as how to dig, clean and identify finds. These and other important tips and tricks are vital if you want to succeed as a future metal detectorist.

Choosing a metal detector

The most important thing to know here is that there is no "right" or "best" metal detector. It all depends on what you're hunting for, where you live, your budget and your experience level. The general rule of thumb is to start with an entry-level metal detector then work your way up. Let's take a look at the most important factors to consider:

What you're hunting for – Many metal detectors out there have been made for specific types of hunting.

1. There are metal detectors specifically designed for **finding gold**
2. Although all metal detectors can technically detect gold, the problem is that gold is most often found in heavily mineralized ground (filled with magnetic iron particles or with conductive salts or both) and a lot of metal detectors will keep falsing when used in these

conditions. Entry-level detectors are not very useful in this case and you need a detector made for finding gold.

3. Metal detectors for **hunting beaches**. You can use an entry-level metal detector for beaches and if it's a freshwater beach then you just need to make sure your detector can get wet. But if it's a saltwater beach you will need a detector designed for this specific purpose otherwise you will keep getting false signals. Beach detecting is discussed in more detail later on.

4. **Relic** metal detectors. Most relics are also found in mineralized ground but using a gold or beach detector for these is problematic since most relics are made of steel, brass or iron and respond well to relic metal detectors that use low frequencies which are effective in finding these specific metal types. However, many modern metal detectors offer

different modes for finding different types of metals.

5. Metal detectors for **hunting coins**. Although almost any metal detector can find coins, there are some detectors that are superior in their coin-hunting abilities and usually offer high-quality discrimination for filtering out metals like iron that might be masking the coin.

6. **Underwater** detectors. This is not a common category and most people don't need these but they are specially designed for finding metals deep underwater. Even though standard waterproof metal detectors can be used in water, these underwater detectors are mainly for hunting at great depths under high water pressure.

7. **Multipurpose** metal detectors. These use a range of frequencies to find coins, relics and precious metals and some even work in highly mineralized ground conditions. The

disadvantages of these are the price and the fact that all the extra functions they have mean you have to spend more time learning how to use all the bells and whistles.

Where you live – As we've already discussed, many metal detectors are specialized based on the ground conditions they are going to be used in. If there aren't any beaches where you live or the ground isn't highly mineralized you obviously shouldn't buy a metal detector designed for hunting metals in those conditions.

Budget and Experience– You can get started with an entry-level metal detector for around $100-$300 or you can invest in a mid ($400-$1500) or high-end metal detector (some go up to $10,000). There are some important things to consider here.

First of all, an entry-level detector is completely fine when you're starting out and you'll be able to find a lot of items with it. There's no point in spending a lot of money when you've never tried metal detecting before and you're not sure whether you'll like it or not.

Secondly, more expensive metal detectors do, of course, offer more functions and precision. For example, an entry-level detector might not be able to detect a coin that's buried next to a piece of iron, whereas a mid-level detector will be able to pick up two separate targets. A high-end detector might be able to provide much deeper detection, advanced target separation, a visual target ID, a large range of frequencies for multipurpose detection, etc.

However, there does certainly become a point when detectors above a certain price are practically pointless and don't offer any significant advantages compared to lower priced detectors.

So, overall, it is best to buy something you can afford and not spend too much on your first metal detector till you're sure you want to continue with this hobby.

There are 3 major kinds of metal detectors:

- Beat-frequency oscillation. These are the oldest, simplest, and cheapest metal detectors. Nowadays professional metal detector manufacturers don't make this type of metal detector.

- Very Low Frequency (VLF). Very versatile detectors that can be used for different types of metals in different ground conditions.

- Pulse Induction (PI). These are commonly used for finding gold and are the best for highly mineralized ground conditions. They can find targets buried deep down and outperform VLFs in saltwater and other ground conditions where mineral levels are high. They can effectively ignore hot rocks and conductive salts. The downside to PI detectors is that they don't discriminate trash very well and if the area you're hunting has a lot of cans and nails or other junk scattered around the ground, you will have difficulty hunting.

Regardless of all the factors mentioned above, there are some features that you should look for when buying a metal detector. A cheap and completely basic metal detector will quickly lead to disappointment and frustration since you'll only be able to find very obvious targets that are close to the surface of the ground as well as the added annoyance of constant falsing, not to mention the fact that you'll be wasting time digging up trash.

So here are the most important things you want your metal detector to have:

Discrimination (absolutely necessary to have) – This will help your machine to ignore (or notch out) junk or metals you don't want to find. It's not always accurate but it definitely helps keep useless digging to a minimum.

Sensitivity (absolutely necessary) – Being able to adjust your detector's sensitivity based on your hunting location is crucial. In an area where there is electrical interference you want to be able to crank down the sensitivity (unless you want to get *chatter* – which can ruin your entire hunt). The same goes for when you're hunting in mineralized ground.

Target ID (necessary) – Helps you get an idea of what you've found. Again, it's not accurate 100% of the time, but it is right more than 50% of the time.

Tone ID (preferable) – Many metal detectors offer different pitched beep tones for different types of metals. If your metal detector only has one tone, you've got no choice but to dig up everything you come across to see what it is. With different pitched tones, you know what type of metal you've come across. For example, many metal detectors have a high-pitched tone for silver whereas low-pitched tones usually (not always) indicate gold or platinum.

Depth Indicator (helpful for beginners) – Although many experienced metal detectorists learn to gauge the depth of their target based on the strength of the beep tone, beginners will benefit from this feature. Essentially, it approximately lets you know how far down the target is.

Automatic ground balancing (preferable) – This feature allows your detector to automatically ignore false signals from mineralized ground and detect actual targets. Since the level of mineralization is different in different locations, your detector needs to adjust to the specific conditions of that area and automatic ground balancing makes it much easier than manual balancing. Although useful, this is not an essential feature and you'll be able to find lots of great stuff without it.

Pinpointing (nice to have) – The traditional method of pinpointing is described in the *Terminology* section and involves manually finding the point where the signal is the strongest. This often takes some time and effort so automatic pinpointing is helpful.

Multiple modes (nice to have) – Some metal detectors come with preset modes which you can use to notch out specific metal types.

Waterproof (not necessary) – You only need this if you're going to be hunting in rivers or beaches where the device is likely to get wet. Otherwise you don't need this feature and it's only going to add to the price of your metal detector.

To sum up this chapter, when buying a metal detector the first thing you need to do is decide what you're hunting for. Then you want to make sure the detector is suitable for the area you live in (or plan to hunt in). Finally, you should factor in your budget and choose a detector that's affordable and not too expensive (but not too cheap either).

You definitely want to make sure that most of the features mentioned above are included (at least the ones that are labelled necessary). Below are some of the best metal detector brands on the market today (in random order to avoid the endorsement of any specific brand):

- Garrett
- Minelab
- Fisher / Fisher Lab
- Bounty Hunter
- Teknetics
- XP
- Tesoro
- White's

Equipment

This is not a full list of all the equipment you might need, nor is it a list of accessories that might come in handy (this is discussed in another chapter). Instead these are the tools that you absolutely must have with you when you go metal detecting.

1. **Digger** - Once you've located a target with your metal detector, you need to dig it up and you're not going to dig with your hands right? This is where a digger comes in.

   These function like a shovel, and in some cases an ordinary shovel will do just fine. But depending on where you plan to hunt, you might want to use a specialized shovel. For example, beach scoops are used when you want to go hunting on a beach. There are portable handheld shovels called hand diggers that are used for metal detecting and feature a serrated edge. These may seem like unimportant differences but in reality you need the right tool for the job otherwise you're going to spend a lot more time digging than you should and it's very likely you'll end up with a sore back. It's a good idea to invest in a high-quality digger since you're always going to be using it and you don't want it to break during a hunt.

2. **Pinpointer** – Not an absolute necessity at first but they do make the job much easier once you know the approximate location of the target. Think of it as a handheld metal detector that quickly locates the target with high precision once you've dug your hole.

3. **Probe** – You won't need this if you're not going coin shooting but if you are, this tool will allow you to professionally remove the coin from the ground without doing any

digging. It looks like a screwdriver but without a sharp end (so you don't damage the target) and might not even be made of metal in many cases.

Hunting Locations

Now that you know the lingo and you've got your metal detector and equipment it's time to choose a good place to hunt. In reality, there is no "bad" place to hunt since you never know what might have been there (or happened there) centuries ago or what someone might have dropped from their pockets just a few minutes ago. But there are some places that often have the most treasure. In this chapter we'll cover all of the best locations to go metal detecting and later on we'll single out some of the more common ones and dive into the details of hunting in those specific places.

Your own backyard/garden

This is the first, most recommended place to start for a number of reasons.

Firstly, you truly don't know what might be hidden in your own yard or what used to be there before you moved there (or a hundred years ago) and many detectorists have found valuable items buried in their yards (including gold).

Secondly, it's close and convenient as a place to start your new hobby. Thirdly, you don't need permission to hunt there (getting permission to hunt is discussed later on). Finally, it's one of the quickest ways to get used to using your metal detector in real life. You'll figure out the functions and controls, how to hold it and move it for maximum comfort and efficiency, and all in all it serves as great practice.

Parks

The general idea behind most of these locations is – treasure can be found in areas where a lot of people usually go/have been in the past. Parks are a great example of this, since lots of people go there to play sports or games, walk their dogs, have picnics, attend concerts, etc. and in the process some are bound to lose coins, jewelry and other items. To maximize your chances of finding something try to search in areas where people probably gathered such as: playgrounds, benches, picnic tables, kiosks, under trees and so on. Chances are even higher if you go hunting after a large event like a concert.

Beaches

Some of the best stuff has been found on beaches and you'll see this location at the top of any metal detecting location list. They never get old as tourists and locals visit beaches every year and lose a lot of items especially whilst swimming or playing games. The cold temperature of the water causes the swimmers' fingers to contract and their rings easily slip off. Necklaces are also prone to falling off when swimmers do the breaststroke. Many items are also lost on the beach and not in the water, specifically near the towel lines (where people lie down to sunbathe).

On top of that, the tide routinely washes lost items ashore, not to mention the fact that storms and erosion constantly change the topography and uncover long-lost valuables. Beach detecting does have certain subtleties that you need to learn – not every metal detector will work here, there are specific places to identify and search, there are good and bad times to go hunting and beach detecting has its own special terminology. All of this is discussed in detail in the next chapter.

Fields

This refers to all types of fields but especially fields that are used (or were used) for farming. Many relics, caches and coins have been found in farmer's fields and if the land has any historical significance your chances of finding an ancient artifact are even higher. The best time to hunt farmer's fields is after they have been plowed since this brings buried items up to the surface and increases the likelihood of finding valuables.

Battlefields

A subcategory of fields, there are many battlefields across the U.S., Europe and all around the world which are home to old coins, muskets and other weapons, arrowheads, tools, buttons, buckles and other ancient relics.

Woodland (and footpaths)

These are great places to search for both modern and ancient treasure. Footpaths are frequently used by hikers, joggers, cyclists and others making it a good place to search for stuff that might have fallen out of their pockets. You can also stray from the footpath and search deeper in the woods where you might uncover ancient war relics. Shotgun shells, old bullets, military badges and coins are very common finds in woodlands.

Stadiums, sports grounds, fairgrounds/circus grounds

A lot of distracted people moving around, jumping up and down, regularly reaching into their pockets to pay for beverages, food, tickets and whatnot means a lot of coins and jewelry falling onto the ground. It's best to search near the admission gates, booths and stands, as well as the locations where the vendors most likely sold items. The probability of finding something good is at its highest after a large event. You may also find toys, prizes and other non-metallic objects that could come in useful.

Old churches and churchyards

Since churches usually stay in the same place for hundreds of years this means a lot of activity has taken place there over the centuries, with people regularly attending mass or going to pray, visiting the deceased in adjacent burial grounds or religious ceremonies that could have taken place in the area.

This means there are old coins, trinkets and artifacts to be found near churches. But make sure you don't go hunting in the actual burial grounds near the headstones as this is wrong for several reasons.

Schools and college campuses

You may have to wait till the holidays to get access but there's a lot to be found here. Older schools and college buildings may offer ancient artifacts, especially if they've been around for a hundred years or longer, but even if all the schools and campuses are modern buildings in your area, there's still quite a bit of clad to be found. The best areas to look are the sports fields, bleachers and anywhere else you think students may have congregated or hung out. You will need permission for searching schools and campuses.

Rivers, creeks, brooks and lakes

Gold nuggets, coins and other lost items are usually washed ashore with the current and river banks and shores are a great place to search for items the tide may have washed up. In shallow areas where the stream slows down a lot of minerals are also deposited near the banks. Waterproof metal detectors are required in this case. If you search in the right place, there's a very good chance you might find very small pieces of gold.

Fishing spots

Again, this is a location where people regularly go (and have gone in the past as well, since good fishing spots remain a reliable place to fish for many years) and the most common finds in these places are fishing sinkers and lures, coins, knives, and once in a while you might even come across a fishing pole.

Deserted/Ghost towns and abandoned sites

The downside to these locations is that many detectorists have already searched them but the good news is that these areas are filled with valuable items and you can be sure that not everything has been salvaged. The town may have been used for trade or mining which means a significant amount of coins and gold were exchanged in that area. The people living there might have also left their possessions behind or stashed money in secret places that are waiting to be found.

You can search marketplaces, saloons, and pretty much any other old building. Hollow walls and floorboards should also be scanned as there may be a hidden cache or treasure trove underneath. Abandoned mining camps are also a great place to look but entering one is dangerous and necessary precautions must be taken and extra safety gear may be required. Other abandoned sites include old stone quarries, railroad stations and junctions, and abandoned cemeteries.

Other miscellaneous locations include: camping sites, piers, historical landmarks, bridges, near fence posts and rails, old barns, flea markets, racetracks, any type of reunion area, swimming holes, lookout sites (especially if there is a coin operated telescope), resorts, roadside rest areas, waterfalls, old castles, underneath old trees and demolition sites.

Disaster sites are also well-known hunting sites but you should make sure not to go hunting if the disaster took place recently. These include shipwrecks, plane crash sites and hurricane/tornado paths.

How to Hunt

So you've arrived at the field or beach (or other location) you want to hunt. What's the first step? The first thing you do is divide the field into smaller, more manageable lines or boxes (gridding).

Gridding - If it's not a large field or if there are objects you can use as mental markers then you can do this in your head. If not, you can use stones or other objects lying around to make borders to serve as grid lines. The point of this is to make it possible to methodically search the area without missing any spots. An easy way to grid is to just divide the area into rows and walk up one row scanning the ground then when you reach the end of that row you transition over to the next row and go down that one and repeat this process till you've covered the entire area (illustration below).

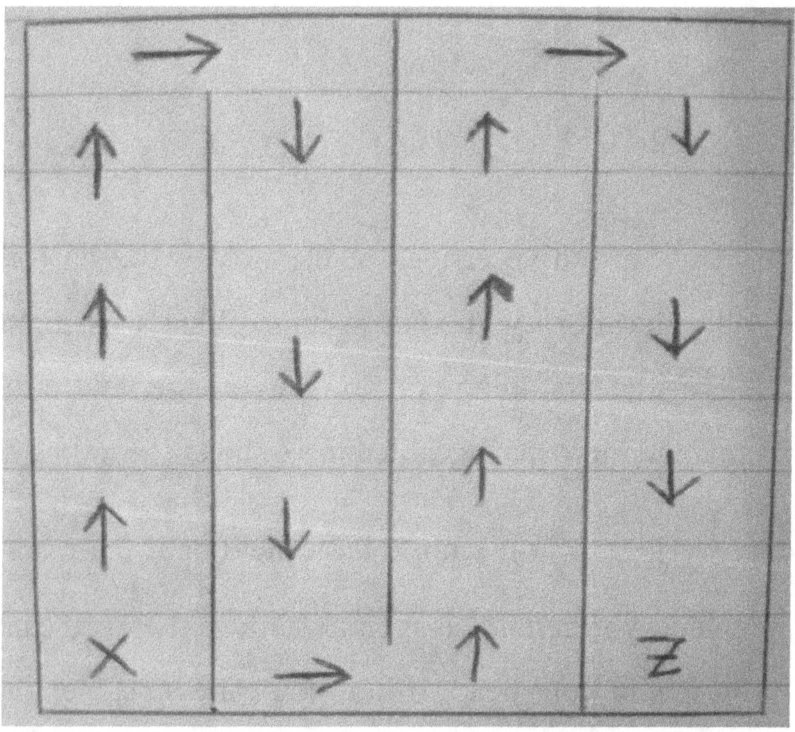

Picture 1. Example of gridding

If you were starting at point X you would follow the arrows through each row till you reach your target Z. By moving through the rows in this manner you can ensure that you've scanned every inch of the area. There is no one-size-fits-all method for gridding and you can improvise based on your location.

Another method that's used is the spiral. In this case you begin from the spot you've found a target and scan in an outwards spiral from that area. This method is employed when you suspect that multiple targets may be in close proximity to each other. But in other cases this method is not as effective as gridding since you miss out on different areas you could've scanned.

Pinpointing – Once your metal detector passes over a target and beeps you need to know where exactly to dig (unless you want to make a huge hole). If your detector has a large coil then that means it covers more ground and usually detects items that are buried deeper (in comparison to small coils) but also decreases precision when it comes to finding the exact location of the target. A smaller coil on the other hand narrows down the target location much better. Either way you need to pinpoint the spot where you're going to dig your plug.

If your metal detector has a pinpoint feature then you're lucky. For each and every metal detector you need to read the user manual to be able to operate all of the features (including pinpointing) properly. The pinpoint mode usually works in two ways:

1. Audio pinpointing – When the coil is directly above the target your detector emits a loud tone and as you move the coil away from the target the tone gradually gets quieter. In this case you sweep your metal detector around the target till you find the place where the

tone is loudest. Sometime metal detectors have an alternative version of this where the pitch of the tone changes as you get closer to your target.

2. Visual pinpointing – The other way your metal detector can let you pinpoint is by visually showing you how close you are to the target on a screen (this can be a number which increases/decreases as you get closer or a radar-like map, etc.)

If your metal detector doesn't have a pinpointing mode there's no need to worry. There is a simple manual method of doing it. Imagine you're standing in front of the area where your metal detector beeped (you're standing on the green **X** illustrated below). You know the target is somewhere in front of you (the grey cross). All you have to do is move the coil from left to right over that area (sweeping motion – the black arrows illustrated below) till you find the spot where the signal (the tone) is the strongest. After you've found it you then move the coil front to back (forwards + backwards) over the same area (the blue arrows illustrated below) till you find the strongest signal again. The point where both signals are the strongest (where they cross) is the location of the target (red star).

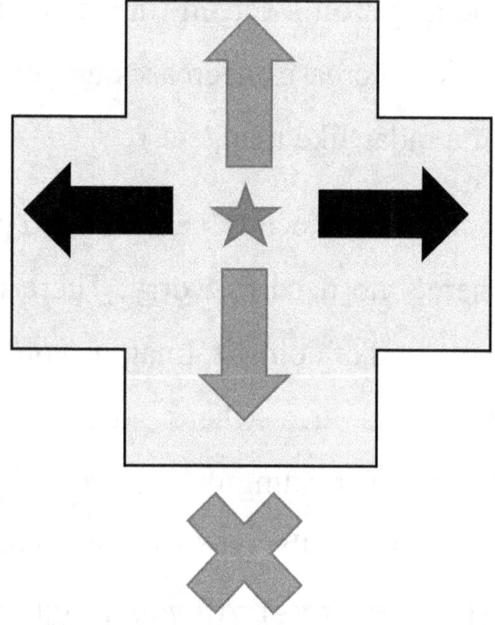

Figure 1. Manual pinpointing

Another way of doing this (which is pretty much the same thing) is sweeping side to side to find the strongest signal then turning 90 degrees and sweeping again to find it again and identifying the point where the strongest signals cross. The only difference is basically the fact that you turn 90° rather than just moving the detector back and forth. When you turn and do the side-to-side sweep it essentially does the same function as the front to back scan in the first method.

These pinpointing methods are also handy when you come across a weak signal and you're not sure whether you should dig or not. Using the pinpointing methods you can try to find out if the signal gets stronger nearby. If the signal remains weak then you can increase the sensitivity of your detector and try again.

In general, those who are new to metal detecting or those who've bought a new detector should dig up any target they find. This is because it takes time to get used to the sounds of each individual machine and the quickest way to know what sound means what is to dig up anything you find. After a while you'll know how your detector responds to different metals in different ground conditions whilst operating under different modes. Once you reach that point, you can confidently skip targets that you're sure aren't worth digging up.

Some important things to keep in mind are:

1. **Take your time** when you go hunting, especially if you're new to this. If you move too fast you will miss certain areas and your detector may get confused and start falsing. It's better to go slow and scan everything.

2. Related to the first point, **make sure your sweeps overlap** so you don't miss any parts in between your sweeps.

3. **Don't bump your coil** onto the ground when you're scanning unless you want to damage your machine or get false signals.

4. Never swing your metal detector like a pendulum when you're scanning. What this

means is **your coil should always remain parallel to the ground** when you move it side to side (illustration below). Neither end of the coil should rise at an angle. Always keep your coil in a horizontal position. If you swing it like a pendulum you will lose many targets and this is actually quite a common thing with new detectorists. Remember to keep your coil close to the ground when you search.

Figure 2. Keeping the coil parallel to the ground

Now that you've successfully found and pinpointed a target it's time to get it out of the ground. There's one main way to do this and that is to cut a plug. There are several types of plugs but they all work the same way. You can have cone-shaped plugs or square/rectangular shaped plugs, you can have plugs with or without a "hinge". Let's start with the classical cone-shaped plug with a hinge.

Cone-shaped + hinge

This is the standard plug you'll see in most metal detecting books and guides and it's effective for targets that are close to the surface (this is where your depth detector comes in). "Close to the surface" is a relative term but it usually means just a couple of inches underneath the surface.

So, let's say you've pinpointed the location of the target and you need to cut a plug. You're standing on the green X (illustrated below) and you've detected a target where the red star is. What you do is kneel down and start digging (or in this case – cutting) a semi-circle around the star (about 4-5 inches away from the star).

The semi-circle is illustrated as the black part of the circle below. You can cut through the soil using the serrated edge of your digger (this is one of the reasons that diggers made for metal detecting are better) or you can stick it into the soil then remove it, then stick it back in next to the original cut and keep repeating this till you've cut your semi-circle.

The side of the digger the serrated edge is on will decide whether you're going to cut in a clockwise or counter-clockwise motion. You can buy a digger that has a serrated edge on the left or on the right side depending on whether you're right handed or left handed.

As you can see below, the circle isn't complete and the part you don't cut is the hinge. Once it's ready you insert your digger into the part of the semi-circle that's opposite the hinge (the part near the green X) and flip the plug out. The plug will now know be on its head but still attached to the ground by the hinge. You want to angle the end of your digger towards the star so that you cut a cone-shaped plug. This makes it easier since the plug is lighter and smaller therefore easier to cut out. If you insert your digger perpendicular to the ground you'll end up cutting a cylinder-shaped plug, which isn't really useful.

Figure 3. Digging a plug with a hinge

Having a towel with you is recommended since you're going to be removing dirt from the ground (especially after you've cut the plug and you begin to look for the treasure) and putting it down on a towel (or some other substitute) will make it easier to fill the hole in once you've found your target.

Once you're done and you've put the dirt back in, the plug itself is popped back into the hole then pressed (using your hands or feet) so it's tightly in place. The point is to make it look like nothing has been dug there. Covering the holes you've made is considered standard metal detecting etiquette and not doing it is rude and can also ruin the scenery of the area (imagine a park or field with lots of holes surrounded by dirt).

Cone-shaped + no hinge

This is used when the target is deep down and you know that after you've removed the plug you're still going to have to continue digging to reach your treasure. In this case a plug that's attached to the ground is just going to interfere and make it harder for you to dig so it's just easier to completely remove it.

In essence, the only thing that's different here is that you cut a full circle rather than leaving part of it untouched like in the first method above. The only problem or downside is that plugs with hinges are a bit easier to pop back in and usually look neater, but that doesn't mean you can't do the same with a plug that hasn't got a hinge.

Square/Rectangular plugs

If you insert your digger straight down and cut your plug in the shape of a square rather than a circle you'll get a square plug. It's going to be heavier than a normal cone-shaped plug and might take a bit longer to cut out. The only upside to having a square plug is that these fit into their original holes the best. If cone-shaped plugs are sometimes visible, square plugs can be placed so well that you won't see them even if you're standing right next to them. It's just a matter of aesthetics really and there's no other reason to opt for a square plug.

One thing to remember is that the type of digger you use depends on the location you're hunting. As we've already mentioned, beach scoops are the diggers used at the beach, there are also relic shovels made specifically for recovering relics as well as improvised diggers. Another thing to take note of is whether or not you can dig large holes in that specific area. Take a field or the woods as an example. You're fine digging huge holes there (but make sure to fill them in) and using large shovels. But compare a field to a park or well-kept garden or yard in the city. Even if you're allowed to dig there (or you're given permission to dig) you definitely can't use the same approach.

Finally, be careful when you dig and always be a bit cautious when recovering items. First of all, it could be a loaded weapon or even an old bomb (it has happened and yes, they can go off). Secondly, it might be a sharp item that could hurt you (such as broken bottles or parts of an aluminum can). Lastly, it could be a very fragile find that you end up ruining by prodding it carelessly or hitting it with your shovel.

You have located the target. You have cut the plug out. Now all that's left is finding the treasure. Your target is either going to still be in the hole that you left underneath the plug, or in the plug itself. So the first thing you want to do is scan the plug with your metal detector. If it beeps then you set the plug onto a towel and begin to gently break it apart. If there is no signal coming from the plug then it's still in the hole. There are several ways to take it from here:

1. You can remove scoops of dirt from the hole using your digger (or your hands) and place it onto your towel and scan the dirt till you find the treasure.

2. If you have a pinpointer (the handheld metal detector we talked about in previous chapters) then this is where it saves the day. You insert the pinpointer into the hole and

move it around till it locates the target with high precision. It's basically a small metal detector that narrows down the target to less than an inch, whereas your main metal detector only pinpoints with a precision of a couple of inches (or more depending on the size of the coil). The pinpointer will either emit a beeping sound or vibrate (or both) when you locate the target. Some will beep faster and faster as you get closer to the treasure. Once you locate it, remember to remove the dirt with caution so you don't damage whatever you've found.

3. If you don't have a pinpointer you can use your metal detector and try to pinpoint where it is in the hole (using its built-in pinpoint feature, or manually). If the coil of your detector is small enough to fit into the hole – even better. Insert it into the hole and try to narrow down the location.

Sometimes an interesting thing happens. After you remove the plug and scan it there's no signal and when you pass the coil over the hole, again, you don't get a signal. It seems as if the treasure has disappeared. There are three possible reasons for this:

1. *The halo effect* – You should already be familiar with this word from the terminology section but in short – metallic objects that have been buried for a long time sometimes generate a field that amplifies the signal coming from the object. When you cut the plug out or dig into the hole you disturb the field and the amplification stops. In this case you just need to continue searching in the hole (preferably with a pinpointer) till you find the treasure.

2. The object has sunk deeper into the soil while you were digging. This is quite common if the soil is soft or if you're digging in sand

(e.g. at the beach). In this case it will keep sinking deeper and deeper till it reaches a hard or rocky layer. It's up to you how long you want to continue trying to recover an object in this case, but if you've been digging for hours or the hole is ridiculously large then it's probably best to fill it up and move on to another location.

3. It was never there in the first place. This is not as common if you are using your metal detector properly but it does happen. It might have been a false signal (possibly as a result of electrical interference or high sensitivity) or you not have pinpointed the target very accurately. You can try to search the immediate surroundings of the hole to see if there really is something there. You may have just dug in the wrong place.

Recovering with a probe

We've already talked about what a probe is (like a screwdriver but with a blunt end, sometimes not even made of metal) and now we're going to discuss when you should/can use one. Probes are only effective for shallow targets (compare the length of your probe to the depth of your target – if the depth of the target exceeds the length of your probe then there's no point using a probe. If it is within reach of your probe, then you can proceed.

Probes are used when you don't want to make a hole in the ground (maybe you're in a park or in someone's backyard and you want to cause minimum damage to the ground) or when the soil is very dry. Dry soil makes it very hard to dig even with a full-size shovel and all you can do is either wait for it to rain or, if the target is near the surface, use a probe.

Probes are generally used for retrieving coins or rings but technically speaking, they can be used for almost any object. To use a probe the first thing you need to do is pinpoint the exact location of the target. Then you insert the probe straight down into the soil (slowly – you don't want to scratch or dent a fragile relic – it could partially or completely lose its value) until you feel the probe touch the target (figure 4).

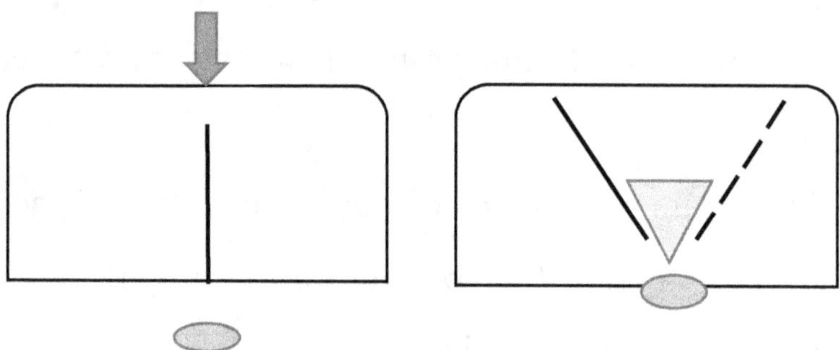

Once it touches the target, take a mental note of the depth (by looking at how far down the probe went) then angle the tip of the probe slightly inwards so the handle faces you (like you would do when cutting a cone-shaped plug) and move the probe in a circular motion to loosen the soil in that part (figure 5). You will end up with a cone-shaped area of loose soil.

The final step is to insert the probe below the target (this is why you needed to remember the depth) and gently push it up through the soil that you loosened till you get it to the surface. Using a probe is not easy at first and requires practice, but once you gain a bit of experience you'll find that it's a valuable skill to have and can save you time and effort as well as allow you to dig in areas you would normally have trouble digging in if you used a standard handheld digger or shovel.

What Settings to Use

As we've already discussed many modern metal detectors have built-in modes to make it easier to detect different types of targets. Each mode has its advantages and disadvantages which we'll look at in this chapter.

All-Metal Mode

As the name suggests, this mode searches for every single type of metal with no discrimination whatsoever. It's a fun mode to use if you want to find a variety of things and don't mind digging out trash as well. Theoretically, this is the only mode that will allow you to find precious metals, coins, jewelry, buttons, ammo and pretty much anything else a metal detector can detect without missing out on anything.

However, this can get annoying if you're searching in an area where there's a lot of trash because you're going to be stopping every few minutes to dig out can slaw or nails. This is why people use discrimination. The all-metal mode also has 2 other advantages: if offers the deepest detection and has a faster recovery speed (explained later) since it isn't doing any additional processing.

Coin mode

This is used for coin shooting and uses a high level of discrimination. In coin mode hot rocks, foil, pull tabs, nails and other small pieces of iron are filtered out so you mainly find coins. However, a high level of discrimination always means an increased chance of missing out on potentially good finds.

Relic mode

This mode uses significantly less discrimination and only filters out small iron objects while accepting all items that do not contain iron. When hunting in fields (especially farm land) many detectorists recommend not going above this level of discrimination as thin silver rings are very close to the iron range and you could end up ignoring them.

This mode is mainly used when looking for old relics.

Jewellery mode

This mode uses a level of discrimination that is between relic mode and coin mode although some metal detectors group coin mode and jewelry mode together under one mode. Jewelry mode is designed to detect rings, bracelets, necklaces and the like that are mainly made of precious metals but can sometimes be made of non-precious metals as well. If it's not grouped together with coin mode, it offers a larger range of metals to be detected but that also means you are more likely to pick up trash every now and then.

Prospecting mode

This is used specifically for hunting gold nuggets or flakes and in locations where there is naturally occurring gold. This mode is not recommended for beginners (unless you bought the detector for gold hunting).

Other than the modes, you can adjust the following settings:

- Discrimination – you can manually increase/decrease it and the higher you go the less objects you'll find (based on their conductivity). Low discrimination means more finds.

- Sensitivity – the higher the sensitivity the deeper you'll be able to detect but there comes a point where high sensitivity will cause continuous falsing as it will begin to detect the minerals in the ground. The key here is balance.

- Notch – this lets you make a window of rejection for certain metals (similar to discrimination but in this case your detector will accept all items below and above that range).

- Pinpoint – if your machine has this mode, entering it will tell the machine to find the exact location of an object. In this case you shouldn't sweep the detector but instead you should slowly move it over the target area and wait for the tone to get louder and reach a peak. This is where the target is.

- Tone ID/Target tone – not all machines have this feature but if yours does you can use it to identify different metals based on the sound your detector makes when passing over it. Since each metal has a different conductivity, this option assigns a tone to different levels of conductivity. For example, if you enable two tones you could have a low tone for gold and a high tone for silver. Some machines use a low tone for iron so you need to always read the user manual. If you set it on one tone this means you'll hear the same tone for every single target you find. If you set it on 3 tones you might have a low tone for gold and nickel, a broken tone for aluminum and a high tone for copper, silver and brass. Some machines offer up to 9 tones.

- Threshold level – again, not all detectors have this but if they do they emit a constant noise or "hum" in the background as you're detecting. Whenever the hum disappears that means you just passed over an item that you rejected (chose to discriminate beforehand). These machines usually offer modulation, which is when the detector emits a faint sound (different from the threshold) to indicate a deep target, and a relatively loud sound for targets that are close to the surface. The threshold needs to be balanced so that it can be heard but preferably as quiet as possible. If the threshold is too low you won't hear the faint signal which indicates deep targets. If the threshold is too high the faint signal will be masked and you'll only hear the loud signal indicating shallow targets.

- GB (may be written differently on different machines) – your ground balancing options. Since the ground can contain minerals which are picked up by your machine, ground balancing automatically adjusts your detector to the mineralization level of the current location so your machine ignores it and focuses on targets. If you choose automatic ground balance, your detector will adjust its settings once, if you choose "*tracking ground balance*" (sometimes written as track/trac or Autotrack) it will adjust to the mineralization level continuously as you scan the location.

- Beach mode – Not all machines have this but this is basically just a mode that, when activated, does ground balancing for the salts in wet sand that you usually find on beaches.

- Accept/Reject – Not all detectors have this (to be more specific this is common for White's detectors). You need to know that each metal has a certain level of conductivity (discrimination works based on these levels). The conductivity of a metal depends mainly on its composition but size and shape also factor in. Based on these (composition + size/shape) there is something called a VDI (Visual Discrimination Indicator). A VDI number ranges from -95 to +95 and each number (or number range) corresponds to a certain type of metallic object. For example, a metal that conducts electricity well (like silver) will be above 90 whereas aluminum foil (which is considered a relatively bad conductor) will be below 10. Negative numbers show metals that are easily magnetized but are bad conductors. Iron or ferrous items (containing iron) will fall in the negative range whereas coins and jewelry mainly fall in the positive range. A VDI number basically tells you what type of metal you've found. You can then choose to reject certain VDI numbers (or a range of numbers) so your detector doesn't beep when you come across those objects. But note that VDI numbers are not guaranteed to be right.

- Volume control – pretty self-explanatory. This is the volume of the sound your machine makes (via speakers or headphones).

- Recovery speed – Most commonly found on more expensive machines. When your metal detector finds a target (or rejects one) it takes a bit of time for it to finish its processing and "recover". Only after it has recovered can it detect a new item. Increasing the recovery speed will allow it to detect new targets quicker but this usually has a negative effect on the depth that it can detect at. If your machine doesn't have this setting then all you need to do is just take it slow and not rush when sweeping.

-

How to hunt specific locations

We've already discussed gridding, sweeping, pinpointing, digging plugs, recovering treasure, using probes and what settings to use. This chapter is going to focus on a few things that you need to pay attention to when hunting in specific areas. Each of the locations listed below has a few unique and distinctive features you need to be aware of.

Hunting fields

If you're in a field that has cultural or historical significance (you can do a bit of research to find out if anything memorable has happened there or if people used to live there) or if you're on a ploughed field, then there are a couple of tips you can follow that may help you find ancient relics. The overall idea is to look for things that seem like they don't belong there or are out of context. These signs usually indicate human activity in the past and mean a higher chance of finding something.

- **Scattered stones** – if you're in a field that doesn't have many stones (or virtually none) then coming across a pile of scattered stones (or tiles) could indicate that a building used to be there in the past. With a bit of experience you can infer what type of building used to be there based on the type of stones you come across as well as how old it probably was. But keep in mind that stones aren't always an indicator of human activity and can just be the result of geological and topographical processes that brought them there. Tiles, on the other hand are definitely man-made and should arouse suspicion. They can be made of granite, limestone, clay or a number of other materials. When in doubt, check it out.

- **Pottery** – Bits and pieces of pottery are also a telltale sign of human activity and a recently ploughed field may have brought a few near the surface for you to see.

- But pottery shards aren't very easy to identify especially if you haven't done any research in that area and the fact that they may be broken up into tiny pieces makes it even harder to distinguish. You may come across pottery ranging from ancient times all the way to medieval times (or even more modern).

- **Seashells** – If you come across any type of shell belonging to sea animals (oysters, mussels, clams, etc.) and there is no sea nearby then humans have almost definitely inhabited that area centuries ago. Oysters, for example, used to be part of people's diets for a very long time starting from a few thousand years ago (possibly even before that). These shells are quite durable and remain in the soil for tens of thousands of years (they're basically fossils). Oyster shells become white/pale over time and this makes it even easier to see them against the color of the soil.

- **Animal presence** – If you come across any type of animal (rabbits, moles, birds, etc.) on a field this could mean that humans have been there before. The logic behind this is that if humans lived there ages ago then a lot of organic waste has seeped into the soil making it fertile. This in turn means lots of worms, bugs and other food for larger animals, making it a good place for birds to regularly come down and hunt and larger animals to permanently settle there. Obviously, if it's a plowed field then you can already assume it is fertile soil (otherwise the farmers wouldn't grow crops there), so this tip mainly refers to fields that aren't being used for agricultural purposes.

A method that some detectorists employ when searching fields when they're short on time is the X (Union Jack) method. In this case they scan the field from one corner to the opposite one diagonally then do the same for the other two corners (making an X). Finally they scan the perimeter of the field. This is just a quick way of seeing if there are any targets packed together or any good spots in that particular field. It is by no means a thorough method as you won't cover most of the area and is only used when you don't have much time. With this method if you come across a good target you then switch to a more methodical method of searching like gridding.

Without exaggeration, there is a ton of treasure to be found in and near streams. In this part whenever we talk about streams the same principles apply to rivers, brooks, and creeks.

These locations have always had (and continue to have) a lot of human activity. Back in the old days some would go to bathe in the water or wash their belongings. Nowadays they go fishing, play in (or near) rivers, have picnics next to the stream, sit next to it just to hear the relaxing babbling of the flowing river or for a million other reasons.

Of course, this also means there may be a monumental amount of trash in the stream (especially if it's close to a busy road). Nevertheless, it's a fantastic place to search. But where exactly do you look? Other than just searching the river bed (which isn't very productive) there are some places where you should definitely look.

The rule of thumb is to look for areas **where the current slows down**. If an object falls into the stream, the current carries it until it reaches a point where the current slows down. Here, the object either falls to the bottom (the streambed) or washes up near one of the banks. Usually, the current slows down where there are large objects in the way (such as rocks and boulders, or man-made objects), where the depth of the stream changes (e.g. suddenly becomes shallow) and wherever the stream changes direction (especially when it's a drastic change/sharp turn).

If there is a bend where the river changes direction you should scan the riverbank closest to where the river bends. If the depth changes you should scan the riverbed in that area (obviously you need a waterproof metal detector). If there is a large object in the middle of the stream then you should scan the area surrounding that it.

Generally, if you see sand or gravel (or any form of erosion) near the banks of a stream you should scan them. This is especially true if the sand/gravel is near an area where the stream changes direction. Sometimes, these areas are underwater when the water level is high then later becomes visible when the water level drops. This is a prime spot to scan since this is where all the heavy metals and minerals deposit. You might even find gold in these areas. You may come across sand or gravel in the middle of the stream as well, if there is a large rock or object close to which they can accumulate. These spots are also worth checking out.

One last thing to remember is eddies. Sometimes when there is an obstruction (like a boulder) in the river and the main current flows around it, a second current is created which flows in the reverse direction. This second current fills the space behind the obstruction and creates a sort of "pool". These pools are mainly found in the inside of the corner where the stream bends and they often have foam bubbles that distinguish them as eddy pools. In the picture below you can see the main current flowing downstream on the right and on the left you can see the eddy swirling back and creating the foamy pool.

The reason that eddy pools are important is because heavy objects that were carried by the current usually fall onto the riverbed where the eddy pool is located. A good way to figure out the direction of a current (and whether it reverses) is to throw in a leaf or blade of grass and see where it goes.

But a word of warning – eddy currents can be dangerous (especially near the line where the two streams separate) and they can knock you over and carry you downstream. The same also applies for non-eddy areas of rivers which have strong currents.

You should also keep in mind that rivers can be much deeper than they seem. Even great swimmers have been known to drown after being hit by a strong current. The rocks and other objects that may be in the river are an additional source of danger. Don't risk your life for any treasure and always use common sense. If you can't tell the depth of the water, don't try your luck. Only search streambeds if the stream is visibly shallow and you can see the bottom (or at least shallow enough for you to step into without risking your life). And again, a shallow stream doesn't guarantee safety. The fact that it's almost impossible to swim in strong currents means you should look at depth and current strength as two completely different sources of danger.

Beach hunting

Metal detecting on the beach is a completely different story. It is definitely worth learning not only because it's fun, but also because the chances of finding valuable items are very high.

Not only can you find plenty of modern jewelry and precious metals but also a considerable amount of old coins and relics, some of which end up on the beach from the depths of the ocean.

On beaches you can expect to find items you wouldn't usually find elsewhere like human teeth (with gold fillings), bullets and cell phones, not to mention a very large variety of trash.

First off, you need to decide what type of metal detector you're going to use. Obviously, it needs to be waterproof and it needs to have the appropriate ground balancing capabilities if it's a saltwater beach.

The two main options are: PI (pulse induction) and VLF (Very-low frequency). PI detectors handle saltwater better and achieve greater depth. Unfortunately, they do not discriminate very well. If the beach you want to hunt has a history of having gold or other precious metals then you can try a PI detector. Otherwise VLF detectors are more convenient as they offer discrimination and will stop you from digging up junk every two minutes. The downside to VLF detectors is that if you crank up the discrimination you might miss some potential targets.

Now where is the best place to search? Firstly, you can **scan the towel line** (where people lie down to relax or get a tan). It's useful to visit the beach while people are still there to understand where the line is. But wait till they leave before scanning that area (you can scan around them but keep some distance and make sure not to get too close since it's not nice having someone get into your personal space and wave a machine around you while you try to relax). Surprisingly, jewelry often slips off as a result of suntan lotion and many people don't even notice. You can also take note of where people are playing football or volleyball and scan those areas as well.

The second place you should look are where there are **cuts**. We've talked about cuts in the terminology section and this is what they look like. Searching along the cut is one of the best ways to find treasure at the beach.

A "cut" in the sand

When a lot of sand is removed by the ocean, buried treasure becomes easier to find. Cuts can be huge (over a couple of feet) or small (a couple of inches).

If you see a part of the ocean that doesn't seem to run parallel to the beach but instead seeps into the beach (the water line seems to be different here compared to the rest of the beach) then you've found a *scallop* (another metal detecting term). Scallops can be seen from a distance (you won't be able to tell it's a scallop if you're standing next to it). These are also a recommended place to hunt.

The general rule of thumb, as we already mentioned in the field hunting section, is to look for areas where something is different. With beaches, this includes places **where the sand has been removed** (cuts), holes of different sizes and shapes, sand pockets and any form of erosion. Places where the sand has been removed offer the best chances of valuable finds since you get access to detect areas which are usually buried deep down.

If you can't find any abnormalities or cuts, and the towel line hasn't helped out you can resort to gridding an area of the beach parallel to the ocean (or perpendicular to the ocean – there's some debate over this) as you would if you were in a field.

If you're hunting on dry sand, choose an area that's close to where everyone is (or was). If you're hunting on wet sand, go for the area where most of the people enter the water. Remember – wet sand has a different concentration of minerals and you need to make sure your detector is suitable for hunting on wet sand. If you're detecting in the water, your best bet is where most of the swimmers were.

An important factor is the tide. First off, you most likely know that when the water level is at its highest, that's a hide tide and when it's at its lowest, it's a low tide. Now, if the tide was high during the day then you'll find a lot of stuff on the beach (specifically the part of the beach the tide was covering during the day) once the tide goes back. The tide will also push objects towards the tide line (the high tide line in this case) so searching that line is a good place to start.

If the tide was low during the day, then you should hunt near the low tide line. Generally, it's best to search the entire area between the high and low tide lines. If you're lucky enough to get a negative tide (when the tide goes back past its "0" or default point), you'll be able to access areas which are underwater most of the time.

Hurricanes and storms can quickly change the topography of the beach and remove large amounts of sand so it's a good idea to go hunting after a storm. But make sure it's safe to go and don't hunt during the actual storm/hurricane.

Seasons also affect the topography of the beach and changes often occur during winter. Strong winds can also have the same effect. Spring and summer are great times to go hunting because of human traffic, whereas winter hunts can be fruitful but only if the sand is moved.

Sometimes the sand will be very mushy (if you're hunting on wet sand) and objects (especially heavy metals) sink to the bottom. The "bottom" is actually a layer of rocks deep below the surface of the beach. You can find treasure in mushy sand, but if you get a signal and start digging and don't find anything the target may have sunk deeper into the sand. These objects will eventually reach the hard, rocky layer below and stop moving. But getting there is hard and not something the average person will attempt.

However, if you are extremely lucky, a strong storm can remove enough sand for you to be able to reach the bottom (which people have claimed is a treasure chest).

Once you locate a target you can figure out how deep it is based on the sound of the beep – if it's loud then the item is close to the surface, if it's a faint signal then you've got something buried deep below. If it's a shallow target use your beach scoop to remove a portion of sand from there. Check the hole with your metal detector. If there's no signal then the target is in your scoop. All you have to do is empty your scoop next to the hole and flatten it out to find your target. If there is a signal in the hole then empty your scoop and dig out a new portion of sand from the same location and check again. The point is to eventually get the object into your scoop which you will know has happened when there's no signal coming from the hole. If it's a deep target you can save some time and remove a couple of scoops of sand before checking to see if it's in the scoop or still in the hole (but it's better to check every time you remove some sand – just to be on the safe side).

When digging in wet sand try to dig quickly so your target doesn't manage to sink further down. If the signal disappears this doesn't always mean the target is gone (or has sunk too far to be recovered). Continue digging and there's a 50-50 chance you'll find it.

Remember that hunting in water is quite difficult for two reasons: sweeping is harder since you're moving against the resistance of the water so you're going to tire quicker and digging is harder because the water quickly pushes sand back into the hole.

There is also the danger of being knocked over by a wave or being carried out further into the depths of the ocean. Wearing a life vest or something similar is recommended and use common sense and don't enter the water if there are strong currents or a high surf (there's usually a flag that indicates the safety level).

 An interesting thing you should know is something called the "*coin line*". If you find coins on the beach (or jewelry, but this mostly refers to coins) try to see if there's a pattern in the locations of those coins. Sometimes the coins are on a line across the beach parallel to the ocean (near one of the tide lines or in-between). If you notice 2-3 coins in a line then keep scanning that line – you're likely to find more. Some final things to keep in mind when hunting the beach are:

- Don't sweep too fast or like a pendulum (explained in previous chapters)
- Don't bump the coil against the sand (to avoid falsing)
- If waves wash over your coil you may end up with false signals
- Don't stick your hand into the sand to retrieve a target as you might cut yourself on a sharp item
- Treasure often turns up after riptides

Cleaning your finds

After you've recovered some treasure, you may be tempted to clean it to see what it is or what markings there are on it. But many of your finds may be very fragile (relics, old coins, etc.) and susceptible to damage. Using the wrong method to clean them (or cleaning them at all) could cause them to lose some or all of their value. This is why you need to know how to clean different types of finds, when to contact a professional to clean it for you and when to just leave it as it is.

Old coins

If the coin seems to be old and may be valuable the first thing you should try to do is figure out how valuable it is. Try to look for markings on it that may indicate what sort of coin it is (identification of finds is discussed in the next chapter).

The main factors that decide the value of the coin are when it was made, how many of those coins were made, and the current condition of that coin.

If you suspect it's valuable or if you can't get any information on it then it is best not to clean it yourself, otherwise you risk damaging it. Imagine finding a coin worth a fortune then losing the opportunity to sell it because you cleaned it carelessly (some ancient coins have been sold for over 3 million dollars!). Even if you don't plan to sell it, it's always better to collect coins that have retained as much of their value as possible. In these cases, it's best to give it to a professional to clean.

If, however, you still want to clean it yourself then the safest way to do it is to put it in **olive oil**. The oil will clean the dirt off the coin without affecting the coin itself, but the only downside to this method is that you have to leave it in the oil for quite a long time (a couple of months). A faster, but riskier, method is to use a soft bristled toothbrush to gently clean the dirt off. Then, if the metal is tarnished, you use **toothpaste** to recover the shine and sparkle of the coin. All you have to do is apply a bit of toothpaste on the coin and gently rub it across the surface. Then you clean it under some warm water and take a look. If it's not as good as you want it to be, then you repeat the process. The toothpaste method is often also used for cleaning jewelry and is quite effective when the jewelry is made of precious metals (with non-precious metals you might not notice any difference). Although the toothpaste method is not considered dangerous in terms of harming the coin, it's not foolproof and may have a negative effect on some coins.

Other methods include using **lemon water** (which contains citric acid) or **vinegar** (contains acetic acid) to clean coins. Beware, both of these can damage the coin, so if you have the slightest doubt that it may be valuable, give it to a professional. One final method you can use is electrolysis which we'll get to in a moment.

Clad (modern) coins

With clad coins you don't have to worry too much. You can use a toothbrush to clean the dirt off, then use warm water and soap to give it a final clean. Another way to go is to put the coins in a jar or bottle of vinegar and shake the bottle before taking the coins out and rinsing them under tap water. Some people also use a rock tumbler to clean their clad and claim it's a very effective method.

Relics

If you've found an ancient relic, much of what was mentioned in the "old coins" section applies. That is – don't clean it yourself if it's valuable and if there's even a 1% chance you might damage it. If you do decide to clean it yourself and the relic is highly oxidized (rusty) then you can perform electrolysis. You still have to clean it with water and soap before starting the process so the risk of damaging it still exists.

Electrolysis can also be used for cleaning the rust off old coins and jewelry. Electrolysis affects the object chemically rather than mechanically making it somewhat safer, but even too much electrolysis can and will damage the object. Here's how effective it can be:

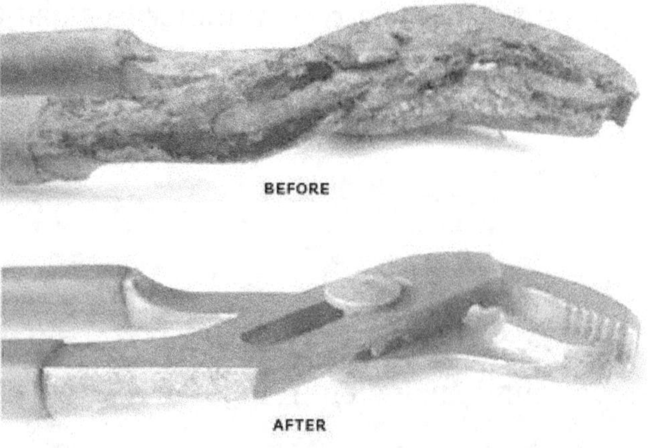

Picture 5. Rust removal with electrolysis – before and after

Electrolysis

So what do you need for electrolysis?

- A non-conductive container (preferably plastic). Some people use buckets, but any other non-conductive container will work

- A piece of uncoated steel or iron. It can be a flat piece or a bar (many people recommend using rebar). This is going to be the anode. Do not use stainless steel as it will create very toxic compounds during the process. Use something you won't mind throwing away later (it's going to rust during the electrolysis)

- A power supply. Low voltage (6V-12V) direct current is recommended which is why car battery chargers are the most commonly used power supply for electrolysis. Make sure the power supply is short-circuit protected

- The object/relic you want to clean (which will also serve as the cathode)

- 2 wires/cables
- Water
- Baking soda
- Tablespoon

To start off, you need to gently clean the relic with warm water, mild soap (make sure there aren't any strong chemicals in it) and a soft brush (although it's sometimes safer to not use a brush and clean it with your hands). The point of this step is to clean off any wax or oil that may be on the relic, which, if present on the relic, will render the electrolysis process useless. Once that's done you can move on to the actual process.

1. Fill the container with water (the water level should be high enough to cover the relic once it's in the container).

2. Then you add the baking soda to the water – one tablespoon of soda for each gallon of water. Stir it up so it dissolves.

3. Place the piece of iron or steel inside the container. It's best to secure it to the

container somehow so it doesn't move around. You should leave a bit of the iron/steel sticking out of the water. This piece/bar of iron or steel is going to act as the anode (the positively charged electrode) and is often called "the sacrificial anode" because it rusts during the process and cannot be used many times (you might be able to use it more than once though).

4. Place the relic inside the container. **Make sure the relic is far away from the iron/steel. If they are close – be absolutely sure that they will not touch!** If they touch each other at any time during the process you will get a dangerous short circuit.

5. Connect the first wire to the relic. The relic is going to act as the cathode (the negatively charged electrode). Connect the second wire to the part of the iron/steel that's sticking out of the water (the anode). The reason you want to connect it to the part sticking out of the

water is so that it doesn't rust (especially if you're using an alligator clip – you don't want to ruin it). Any metal that's underwater and touching the anode is going to rust.

6. The final step is to connect the other end of the first wire (the one that's attached to the relic/the cathode) to the negative side of the power supply and connect the other of the second wire (the one that's attached to the anode) to the positive end of the power supply. You then turn on the power supply and wait.

There is no right amount of time to wait and it mainly depends on the power of your power supply and the relic. It's best to just frequently check up on the relic and see how it's going. After turning on the power supply you should start to see bubbles rising from the relic. If there are no bubbles after 30-60 seconds then turn off the power supply and check the connections. The bubbles are a result of hydrogen gas forming as a result of electrolysis. After a while you may see a reddish-brown froth forming near the surface of the water (and possibly a layer of waste near the bottom of the container as well). This is a good sign and it means the process is working and the rust is getting cleaned off.

Once you think the rust has been cleaned off, turn off the power supply and rinse the relic under some tap water. You can then leave it to dry or use a hairdryer (if it's not a heat-sensitive relic).

Warnings

1. Electricity starts to run through the water once the power supply is on. Do not put your hands in the water whilst the power supply is still on. Do not turn on the power supply until you have completely finished setting up the container, the relic, the iron/steel bar and all the connections. You could get seriously shocked.

2. The bubbles being produced is an indicator of
    hydrogen production. Hydrogen is an
    extremely flammable gas. Do not light any
    fire near the container.

Precious stones

Generally, the best way to clean diamonds, rubies, emeralds or other precious stones at home is to use warm water and mild dish soap.

Identifying your finds

You've got your treasure, you've cleaned it (or not) and now you want to know what it is, or what it's made of and how much it's worth. You might identify your find before you clean it so it's not always in this order. So how do you identify it? It depends on the type of treasure.

Coins and relics

With clad coins, you probably won't have any trouble identifying them after you clean them (unless they're in an extremely bad state).

With old coins you're going to have to do some research. First of all, take a look at the markings and see if you can make out a date, a phrase, or even a single word or any other inscription that could give you a clue as to where it came from or how old it is.

Start by searching the Internet for whatever you found on the coin. If nothing comes up you can take a picture of your coin and attempt a reverse image search (Google offers this service). If that doesn't work either, the next best place to go to is one of the many metal detecting clubs/online communities.

Depending on the country you live in, there may be plenty of local metal detecting clubs in your area which you can find with a quick search on the Internet. If not, you can always try online metal detecting communities. You'll find countless forums and websites dedicated to metal detecting where detectorists share their finds, ask for advice, share tips, and help others to identify what they've found. You'll find lots of detectorists eager to help and when you combine that with the fact that some of them are veterans in this field, you've got a good chance of quickly identifying your find.

On a final note, there are catalogs of coins that contain illustrated pictures of hundreds of coins along with their descriptions that could come in useful. One of the most famous ones is the *"Standard Catalog of World Coins"*.

With relics, most of the steps mentioned above apply, especially when it comes to asking online communities. But there are a few extra steps you can take with relics. Based on the location of where you found the relic, you can research the land and its history, then use that information to figure out what type of relic it might be (e.g. if a battle has taken place there it could be a war relic and related to weapons/armor, belts/buckles or something soldiers might have carried, etc.). You can use this same tip for old coins but it's usually more effective for ancient relics. Another thing you can try is to take your relic to the nearest archaeological unit or museum and ask them to help you identify it.

Jewelry

Real jewelry is usually much easier to identify since precious metals are almost always marked. Whether it's a bracelet, a ring, a necklace or an earring you will find a stamp showing the metal type and its quality. Rings are usually marked on the inside whereas necklaces and bracelets will have the stamp somewhere near the clasp. Earrings are most often marked on the back. You might need a magnifier to see the inscriptions.

For gold you may come across one of the following:

- 10K – this means 10 out of 24 parts is pure gold. In other words it's about 41% gold.

- 14K – 14 out of 24 parts is pure gold. Which means 58.5% percent gold. This is also written as ".585"

- 18K – 18 out of 24 parts is pure gold. That means you've got 75% pure gold. Also written as ".750"

- 20K – 83% pure gold, also written as ".833"

- 22K – 91% pure gold

- 24K – 100% pure gold, also written as ".999"

The part that's not pure gold is an alloy of metals that make the jewelry more durable. Gold is actually a soft, malleable metal and mixing it with other alloys makes it stronger. Jewelry is usually not made with 100% (24K) gold since it won't last as long.

For platinum you might come across these markings:

- PLAT
- PT - sometimes it's followed by one of the numbers below
- 900 – 90% platinum
- 950 – 95% platinum

Platinum jewelry never contains less than 90% pure platinum, and precious metals are used for the other 10% as well. This makes platinum jewelry more expensive than gold, and it has some other advantages as well: it always remains white and rarely tarnishes (unlike gold) and it's hypoallergenic.

For silver you will have one of the following:

- Sterling silver/925 – this means the silver contains at least 92.5% pure silver
- 900 – otherwise known as "coin silver" – it contains 90% pure silver
- 800 – also known as "European silver" or "Continental silver" – these contain 80% pure silver
- Britannia silver/950 – contains 95% pure silver and is softer than sterling silver

You may also come across palladium (PD), tungsten or titanium.

There are several professional ways of checking precious metals (other than checking the stamp). The first, most popular method is an acid test. These can be bought online and most acid test kits contain several bottles of nitric acid (for testing different gold purities). Nitric acid dissolves any metal that isn't gold. This method involves scratching an area of your gold jewelry with a sharp tool to remove the outer lay of gold and expose the inner layers. An inconspicuous spot is chosen so that the scratch can't be seen when wearing the jewelry. Then, a drop of nitric acid is added to the scratched area. If the metal in that spot turns green or fizzes then it's fake gold. If it turns into a milky color, then that indicates silver underneath (the jewelry had a gold plating on top of the base metal which was silver). If there is no reaction/color change you can then clean the jewelry and try to identify the purity of the gold.

Often, acid test kits will have multiple bottles of acid for testing 10K (or 12K), 14K, 18K and 22K gold (sometimes they may have separate bottles for platinum and silver testing as well). The strength of the nitric acid increases with the purity you want to check. In other words, the acid contained in the 22K bottle is stronger than the one in the 10K bottle. To determine the purity 2 methods can be used:

1. Starting from the strongest acid (22K) you apply the acid to the area you scratched and wait for a reaction. If there is a reaction you clean the acid off (the acid is usually cleaned off using a mix of water and baking soda) and try a weaker acid (18K). You repeat this process till you reach an acid strength that doesn't cause a reaction. If, for example, the 14K acid is the one that doesn't cause any fizzing or bubbling or any other reaction, then you've got 14K gold. The downside to this method is that you're eating into your jewelry.

2. Using a testing stone. These acid kits almost always come with a black testing stone. You gently scratch/rub the gold on the stone till you get a line of gold on the stone (this does damage the jewelry so be careful and make it

a small scratch). You then apply a drop of each acid (10K, 14K, 18K, and 22K) to different parts of the gold line and observe which acid doesn't cause a reaction. The one that doesn't corresponds to the purity of the gold you have.

Warning – nitric acid is dangerous so make sure you're wearing gloves and eye protection when performing this test. You should also be in a well-ventilated area as the acid fumes are toxic.

Although this method is very accurate, it can also harm your jewelry, especially if you make a large scratch or pour too much acid on it. Other methods of testing include:

- Using an unglazed ceramic plate or porcelain tile or black testing stone (also called a jeweler's stone). This is similar to the second part of the acid test method but it's much more basic. All you do is scratch the gold on the stone and look at the color. If it leaves a gold streak then it's gold. Black streaks indicate fake gold. This method will also damage your gold since you have to press somewhat firmly against the testing stone for it to leave a streak but if you're not careful and use too much force you could cause some serious damage and end up with an ugly scratch on your gold.

- Density test – You take a measuring cylinder and fill it with water. Take note of the water level before continuing. You then weigh your gold in grams and drop the gold into the cylinder. Record the new water level and calculate the difference between the initial and final water levels (the displacement). For example, if it was 30ml at first then it became 35ml then the difference is 5ml. Finally, you divide the weight of the gold, which you measured earlier, by the displacement (e.g. if the gold weighed 100 grams, 100/5 = 20). This is the density of your gold. The number should be close to 19.3 g/cm^3 which is the standard density of gold. Keep in mind that gold with a lower purity level (e.g. 14K) has a lower density so the number may be in the 12.7-20 range. This method isn't 100% accurate, since your jewelry may be made of metals that have a similar density to gold. But if the number you get is very different from 19.3 then it's definitely not gold.

- Bite test – The idea behind this is that since gold is a soft metal then biting into real gold will leave bite marks. However, biting into gold-plated jewelry will also have the same effect so it's not really accurate.

- Water test – Again, this isn't very accurate but it's a basic way of identifying fake gold. Since gold is heavy, it should sink after being dropped into a glass of water. If it floats, it's fake.

- Finally, a couple of other basic characteristics that gold has are the following: it's not magnetic (if you bring a magnet close to it and it sticks to the magnet it's fake), it shouldn't leave marks on your skin (real gold jewelry will not react to sweat or oil on your skin, if it does then it's fake) and there shouldn't be any discolorations anywhere – if there are, this mostly likely means the jewelry was gold-plated (the plating has a tendency to come off, revealing the base metal below it).

There are also professional gold testing machines which professional jewelers have access to, which can determine the purity of your gold with high accuracy and without damaging it. If you're going to be testing a lot of gold, you might want to invest in an electronic gold testing machine, which are affordable.

On the other hand, XRF machines, which are one of the most professional tools used for testing gold and silver, are quite expensive and most people don't need to invest in one.

Silver testing methods are similar to the ones used for testing gold:

- Before you perform any test, check to see if there's a stamp. If there isn't (or if you think the stamp has been forged, which does happen, but rarely) then you can move on to the following methods.

- Acid tests are also used for checking silver, however the colors that indicate fake silver are different from the colors used to identify fake gold. Generally, if the color changes to red then you have silver, brown and green indicate silver of lower purity and yellow, dark brown and blue indicate other metals. But this may differ from one acid test kit to another so it's best to read the instructions.

- Density test – This test can also be performed for silver, following the exact same steps used for the gold density test. The density should be around 10.49 g/cm^3. Keep in mind this is the density for pure silver and silver alloys will have a different density.

- Bleach test – A drop of bleach is added to the silver. If it tarnishes and becomes black then it is real silver (silver-plated objects will also tarnish so it's not a foolproof method).

- Ice cube test – Real silver has very high thermal conductivity. If you place an ice cube on it, the ice should melt very quickly (you can put a second ice cube next to it to see if there's a difference in the melting speed)

- The ring test – Definitely not the most accurate method, but one that's very popular. If you drop a silver object onto a flat surface it should make a ringing sound like a bell or a high-pitched pinging sound. If it makes a dull sound then it's probably not real silver.

- Finally, silver is also not magnetic, so if it sticks to a magnet – it's fake.

Precious stones

The most prominent category here is diamonds, but that doesn't mean you won't come across emeralds, sapphires, rubies or other stones mounted on jewelry.

In reality, it is very difficult to tell real and fake diamonds apart without any experience. You can use a magnifier to take a closer look as diamonds often have small imperfections within them (the less they have the more expensive they are) but this isn't very easy to do and not a very accurate method for an amateur/someone with no experience in this field.

The most reliable way is to ask a jeweler but if you want to check it yourself, or if you come across a lot of diamond-containing jewelry and don't want the hassle of going to a jeweler's every time, you can buy an electronic diamond tester. One thing you should pay attention to is how it works, the brand and the price. Many diamond testers work by measuring thermal conductivity and checking if it matches that of a diamond. The problem with this is that moissanites (a gemstone that's significantly cheaper than a diamond) have the same thermal conductivity as diamonds so the machine might tell you it's a diamond, when in fact it's a moissanite.

The solution to this is to buy a tester that also checks electrical conductivity (moissanites and diamonds have different electrical conductivities).

Logging

It's considered good practice to keep a record of all your finds along with when and where you found them, how deep they were buried as well as some other details. First of all, it's fun to be able to look back after a while and see a list of all the things you've found. However, what's more important is that keeping a journal of finds helps you identify good hunting locations. After a while, when you look at your journal you may notice patterns and realize that you found a lot of valuable stuff in the same place or in similar places. "Similar places" is not just about the actual geographical locations, but, for example, you may notice that many items were found in a specific part of a field or river (e.g. near a specific type of rock, or at a particular place on the riverbed), or that treasure is easier to find at a certain time of the day at the beach and you can then use that information in the future to search in those places, or at those times of the day when you go hunting in other similar locations.

Metal detectorists often find a good hunting spot which becomes their go-to place, and most of them keep it a secret. You may notice on online metal detecting forums and websites that even when detectorists post their finds they often don't mention the exact location (though not everyone keeps it a secret) and plenty of lurkers try to figure out where that spot is so they can go hunting there as well. Keeping a journal will help you find locations like that, where you can go back multiple times and find more treasure.

Above journal available online

Finally, in some countries, keeping a record of your finds is mandatory (especially in countries where the laws regarding metal detecting and finding relics are stricter). There are a couple of ways you can go about logging your finds. You can buy a metal detecting journal online, you can make one yourself (not at all difficult) or you can even use a mobile application. If you want to log your finds in a notepad you have, you can use a format like this:

Date and Time	Location	Depth	Gear Used	Target Found

The location should preferably include GPS coordinates since you might be out in a field or in the middle of the woods and an address is not going to be accurate or of much use if you choose to come back to that exact spot.

You can use a separate GPS unit but nowadays some metal detectors come with their own GPS. But the simplest way is to just your phone since all modern smartphones have a built-in GPS and it's highly likely (and recommended) that you'll have your phone with you when you go hunting. Try to include as much information as you can about the target and it's even best to take a photo of your find for a number of reasons.

Firstly, if it's an ancient relic you might not be able to describe it very well with words (or at least not as well as you can with a picture). Secondly, its appearance might change after cleaning it, and you may want to compare it to its original state. Finally, you may notice dents, scratches or other damage and not know if it happened after you found it or if it was like that in the beginning.

Metal Detecting Accessories

Other than a metal detector, a digger, a pinpointer (not compulsory but recommended), and a journal, there are some things you should always have with you when you go hunting.

1. **Food and water** – This is sort of obvious but it still needs to be on this list. Unless you're going for a short hunt in a nearby park, metal detecting can take hours and you are going to get tired. Additionally, you may be in the woods or in a field in the middle of nowhere so you need to have something to drink so you can stay hydrated and something to eat to so you have enough energy to continue hunting.

2. **Sunglasses/sunblock** - Whether you're in a field, at the park, at a beach or anywhere else, you're going to be outdoors and under the sun (unless of course you're hunting at night) so you need to stay protected.

3. **Finds bag/pouch** – This is not an essential accessory but it can be really useful once you start finding lots of small items and not knowing where to put all of them. You could put them in your pockets or in your backpack (which is also something you should have

with you but it's not on this list since you will automatically need one to carry all of the other accessories mentioned here anyway) but find bags offer a few benefits.

a) Your pockets don't have unlimited space. Plus, you don't want to mix your finds with everything else that you've got in your pockets (keys, wallet, phone, etc.). The same goes for mixing it with the stuff in your backpack. You could lose your finds and/or they could get damaged by coming into contact with other items you have in your pockets/backpack. A finds pouch lets you keep the items you've found safely and separately.

b) Finds bags have separate pockets for sorting out your coins, jewelry, relics and whatever else you come across. This makes it easier to prioritize and sort your finds (e.g. precious metals, potential junk, unknown objects). Many pouches also have padded pockets for storing fragile relics which could otherwise get damaged.

4. **Mobile phone** – Again, this is an obvious one and you will probably have one with you anyway. But other than being used for calls (which may come in handy since metal detecting can take you to places where you never thought you'd be), it also doubles as a GPS, a camera, a potential journal for finds and a flashlight. If you're going to be hunting near/in water you will also want to take a waterproof case with you.

5. **Knee pads** – Every time your detector beeps and you decide to see what it is, you'll be getting down on your knees to dig. You can live without them but they provide comfort and protection, especially if you're digging in rocky conditions.

6. **Gloves** – They will keep your hands warm when you're digging in the cold, they'll make it easier to handle your digger and most

importantly, they will keep your hands from getting cut by sharp metal objects (which is a common occurrence). Remember to stay up to date on your tetanus shots.

7. **Comfortable clothes and appropriate footwear** – Since metal detecting is an activity that can take hours and includes moving around, kneeling down and digging, it's best to wear clothes you'll be comfortable in. Try to wear long pants and long-sleeved shirts when you're hunting to avoid bugs and ticks. It will also protect you from getting scratched by brambles and other prickly shrubs. Your shoes should also be comfortable (as you might be in them all day) but they need to protect your feet from sticks, rocks, wires, broken glass and other hazards too. This is why it's best to wear hiking boots if you're going to be in a field or in the woods.

8. **Batteries** – Many metal detectors use standard store-bought batteries (e.g. double AA) while others use rechargeable battery packs. Either way it's always a good idea to have some spare batteries with you since you don't want your detector turning off in the middle of the forest or elsewhere, effectively ruining your hunt.

9. **Towel** – This was mentioned in the *"How to hunt – digging a plug"* section. You need it to collect the dirt in one place so you can fill the hole once you're done.

10. **Support harness** – If your metal detector is relatively heavy or you're going to be out all day hunting you may benefit from using a metal detecting support harness. These distribute the weight of the detector evenly over your body so your arms don't ache after a few hours of hunting.

11. **Flashlight** – Although your phone can function as a flashlight, a strong torch can be

useful for checking holes and looking underneath plugs. If you're hunting at night then it's a necessity.

12. **Coil cover** – Not a vital accessory, but recommended if you've bought an expensive detector. Over time, coils get damaged from being scraped or bumped on the ground or other hard surfaces (especially if you hunt in rough, rocky terrain). Coil covers are inexpensive, usually made of plastic, and they protect your coil from wear and tear, thereby extending the life of your detector (without affecting its functionality/detection depth).

13. Other miscellaneous, non-vital accessories include:

  - Different sized coils (if your detector has them) that you may want to use for covering a large area quickly, or for narrowing down the location of a target,

- Headphones – these can make it easier to hear faint signals,
- A waterproof cover for your control box in case it rains (many detectors have a waterproof/water resistant coil but a non-waterproof control box),
- A compass – as part of a survival kit if you get lost in the woods and can't get a signal on your phone.
- Tear gas or some other form of protection if you're hunting alone.

The Legal Side of Metal Detecting

One of the most important things to remember is that metal detecting can be illegal in certain places. The laws vary from country to country and it's your responsibility to know where you're allowed to go hunting. There may also be differences in federal and state/local laws (in which case federal laws almost always override local laws). Countries also have laws that regulate which finds have to be reported and whether or not you're entitled to it.

For example, in the U.S. different states have different laws regarding the entitlement of treasure troves. Some give the finder the right to keep what they've found, whereas others state that the treasure belongs to the person whose land it was found on (the purpose of this is to discourage trespassing). In most cases, if the treasure is found while the detectorist is trespassing, he/she loses the right to keep it.

Federal laws are governed by the "Archaeological Resources Protection Act of 1979" (ARPA), which states that any archaeological artifact (including pottery, weapons, projectiles, tools, paintings, bottles, carvings, etc.) that is found on public property and is over 100 years old belongs to the government. In England, the "Treasure Act 1996" states that any treasure you find belongs to the Crown. The word "treasure" is defined very specifically based on the age, composition, historical/cultural significance and other factors.

In the UK metal detecting is allowed on most lands if you obtain the owner's permission. Scheduled sites (nationally important archaeological/historical sites protected by the government) require state permission. In Northern Ireland, however, you need permission from the state and the land owner regardless of where you go hunting. The same law also exists in Sweden (which also requires you to report anything you find). Always find out the laws in your area.

Generally, metal detecting is almost always banned (without a permit) on all archaeological and historical sites. National parks are usually off limits as well. Any federally-owned land will require a written permit.

Public property is mostly safe to hunt but it's best to double check since you might end up getting fined (or worse). If you're not sure if you're allowed to hunt in a certain area it's better to just not hunt there since you might not only get a fine, but you could also have all of your equipment confiscated and even end up behind bars (although getting jail time for metal detecting is rare, it can happen).

If you can, always ask whoever is in charge (the ranger at the national park, the priest if you're hunting in the churchyard, etc.). Hunting on school or campus grounds will always require permission from the superintendent or president of the college/university.

When hunting on private property, you'll need permission from the owner. You don't always need a written permit in this case and verbal permission will suffice. Never go metal detecting on private property without asking first. It's not only bad for you but you can also end up giving other detectorists a bad name as well as the hobby itself, which some people think should be banned.

When getting permission from the landowner try to establish trust (a calling card can be helpful in this case) and assure the owner that you're not going to ruin their land. You can ask them if there are any places they don't want you to detect (which shows that you're responsible and ethical) and even agree to show them anything you find. Don't overdo it though, as this may have the opposite effect.

It's very important to be ethical and follow a few rules for both yourself and other detectorists. If you don't follow the rules listed below people will be less likely to grant you, or other detectorists, permission to hunt in the future. Whether you're on private or public property **always make sure**:

1. **You fill in all your holes**. This is the number one rule to remember and the biggest mistake that new detectorists make, as well as the most common complaint land owners have. Metal detecting has been banned in many places because of this. It's rude and disrespectful, and it makes the place ugly. No matter how big the hole is, do your best to put all of the dirt back into the hole and pop the plug back in and press it tightly into place.

   Ideally, no one should be able to tell that a hole ever even existed there and the terrain should look as untouched as possible. This is especially true when you're on private property.

2. **You don't destroy anything**. This is just as important as the first rule. If you have to damage a plant or a tree or even a small shrub to dig out your find, don't do it. The same reasons for rule number 1 apply.

3. **You don't put the trash you find back into the holes**. If you find a pull tab, a rusty nail, a tin or can or any other piece of junk, don't put it back into the hole you dug, collect all the rubbish in a bag then throw it away once you've finished hunting.

4. **You report historical finds**. Of course, it is up to you but this is the most ethical thing to do. Whether or not it's required by law, if you've got your hands on a relic that belongs in a museum it's best to give it to them. You may or may not receive a finder's fee but it's still the right thing to do. That small (or large) artifact could be a very significant cultural/historical find and it's of much more

use in the hands of archaeologists or at a national museum than in your garage.

5. **You leave everything as you found it**. If you had to move some stuff around, open or close any gates, turn something on or off, or change anything else while you were hunting, make sure you change it back and leave it in its original state. The rule of thumb is: nothing should look different once you leave your hunting ground.

Research

Not something that's very fun, but it can be extremely useful. If you know where to look, your chances of finding something valuable double.

If you go out to a random field and start hunting you may or may not find something worth keeping. But if you go to a field which you know served as a battlefield centuries ago, you've got a much better chance of finding an ancient war relic. The same goes for any other land which has a history.

By doing a bit of research you also make it easier to identify any artifacts you may find in that area (e.g. if you're out detecting in a battlefield and you know exactly what battle took place there, you'll know how old the button or bullet you found is and where it came from).

1. Start by researching historical events that took place in your area (or close by). This doesn't mean you should limit yourself to just researching battles. Search for any event where a lot of people participated (e.g. celebrations, gatherings, large public events, etc.). However, you might find that many of those places which used to be empty land now have buildings on top of them, so you can cross those off your list. Focus on the areas where roads and buildings haven't been

built on top of the land where those events took place.

2. Look at old maps of your city (or wherever you are hunting) to see where the buildings used to be. You will be able to find maps like these online or at a local library.

If you can find a spot of land where there used to be a market, a store, a school or anything else and is now empty, that's a good place to search.

You may also find old maps at your town's municipal office. Plenty of valuable information can also be found at local museums. By looking at the displayed artifacts and reading about where they were found (if they're local relics), you can figure out a few locations worth hunting.

3. The Internet. First off, you can take a look at online metal detecting communities and see if any other detectorists have shared any of their spots or recommended any locations. If you do decide to check out someone else's location, always ask them first so you don't "steal" their spot. Most detectorists keep their spots secret but others might gladly invite you along. Always remember to ask.

Secondly, use Google Earth to get a satellite view of your surroundings. It's a very effective way of finding unexplored areas near your house and around the city (or outside the city). You may find fields, hidden footpaths, woods or other places you didn't even know existed. You can also use it to check if a building that you found on an old map has been replaced with something else or if it's just empty land waiting to be searched. You can use the Internet to find old maps as well.

If you live in the U.S. an interesting Internet tool is historicaerials.com which allows you to compare modern and old maps. You can choose a location and view the map of how it looks now. Then you can overlay an older map (you choose how old) on top of that and see what's changed. You can also check out oldmapsonline.org which is quite similar.

4. Often an overlooked strategy – asking the elders in your community. They may be able to impart priceless knowledge and save you a lot of time by telling you where different buildings used to be.

5. Metal detecting/treasure hunting magazines and books. You can find some of these magazines online and there are some treasure hunting books on Amazon which not only teach you how to meticulously research an area before hunting but also have many recommended locations for you to try. Some of those locations may have restricted access or require a permit.

Terminology

First things first, the world of metal detecting has its own unique terminology that you need to know to make things easier in the long run. You'll come across these words not only in this guide but also in practically every other metal detecting book or article as well as the user manuals of different metal detectors.

Air test – After buying a metal detector people sometimes swing different metallic objects in front of the detector to test it. This procedure is known as an air test.

All metal – This is a setting found on many metal detectors which basically means the detector will detect every type of metal it comes across (as opposed to the "discrimination" setting which filters out certain types of metals).

Arm cuff – This is the semi-circular part of the detector that allows the user to secure the metal detector around their arm. Usually features a hook-and-loop closure and padding for comfort.

Artifacts – Old items that have cultural or historical significance (but may not have monetary value). Also referred to as relics.

Beeping – The sound a metal detector makes when passing over metal. Some metal detectors beep only when passing over metal, others beep constantly and begin to beep differently when passing over different targets or become silent.

Black sand – Different types of black sand exist, but one of them features a partially magnetic mixture of elements that are found in *placer deposits*. Valuable minerals accumulate in placer deposits and gold is often found here, along with other precious metals, rare earth elements and even gemstones (diamond, sapphire, ruby, etc.). However, since the ground is heavily mineralized and contains iron oxide, many metal detectors are unable to function in these conditions.

Cache – Several (potentially valuable) items all stored in one place. This can include jars or boxes of coins, jewelry or ancient artifacts. There have been many cases of people finding caches of weapons or ammunition as well.

Can Slaw – Pieces of aluminum cans in the ground that cause your metal detector to beep. These are annoying and can result in a detectorist wasting their time digging up useless pieces of junk.

Chatter – Meaningless noise made by the metal detector when its sensitivity is set on "high" and the ground is mineralized or there are stray electrical signals in the area. Usually fixed by *ground balancing*.

Clad – Coins which have a core and an outer layer made of different metals. All modern U.S. coins are clad. Used synonymously with modern coinage.

Coil – The round or oval shaped part at the end of the metal detector that you move across the ground to detect metal.

Coin shooting – A type of metal detecting that focuses on just finding valuable coins.

Coin spill – When multiple coins are found in the same place close together. Usually a result of coins falling out of someone's pocket.

Control box – The part of the metal detector that contains the circuitry and controls as well as the screen (if the detector has one). The speaker is also placed in the control box. More expensive metal detectors have many extra functions on their control boxes compared to low-end detectors.

Cut – A term used when metal detecting on the beach. The "cut" is a line across the beach where a noticeable amount of sand has been removed by the ocean and as a result the beach has a sharp (or sometimes gradual) slope along the cut.

Dateless – A coin that for different reasons (oxidization, wear) doesn't have a visible date.

Digger – One of the essential accessories of any metal detectorist. Once you've found a target you need to dig it up. This is done with a digger, which is basically a type of shovel. Diggers that are designed for metal detecting usually have a serrated edge on one side that's used for cutting up roots whilst digging.

Discrimination – A setting that many metal detectors offer. Discrimination allows the metal detector to ignore certain types of metals and only look for specific metals. This is very helpful when you don't want to waste time digging up junk (like can slaw or foil) every time your metal detector beeps. However, you need to be careful since too much discrimination can result in you not finding items that could prove to be valuable.

Falsing – When your metal detector beeps but there is nothing to be found. This is usually either because the user is not handling the detector correctly (swinging too quickly or bumping it against the ground) or because of electrical interference (mobile phones, power lines, etc.)

Gridding – The process of dividing a large area into smaller sections to make it easier to search and to ensure you don't miss any spots. You can divide the area into small sections in your mind or you can use sticks or stones to mark the grid lines. Archaeologists often use strings attached to posts when gridding.

Ground balance – In some locations the ground may contain a high level of minerals that interfere with detection since they act like a metal and cause your detector to beep (*falsing*) and mask actual targets. For example wet beach sand contains a lot of salt and red earth contains iron particles. Ground balancing is similar to discrimination and is the process of adjusting your metal detector to the mineralization of the ground at your current

137

location. Depending on the metal detector, ground balancing may be done manually or automatically. Some metal detectors also offer "tracking ground balance" which continuously adjusts the ground balance settings while you are detecting to provide the most accurate readings.

Halo effect – When a metallic item has been buried for a long amount of time, as a result of ionization, it sometimes creates a field or "halo" around it which amplifies the signal produced by the target when you pass your detector over that area. The signal may be strong at first then get weaker as you dig further down (since the field is disrupted). Some people assume that they had a false signal at this point but they will eventually find the target.

Hot rock – Rocks that contain iron compounds and cause your detector to beep. These rocks don't contain valuable metals (e.g. gold or silver) and can usually be filtered out with discrimination.

Hunting – Same as metal detecting.

Iron masking – This is when a piece of metal is right next to a valuable target and your metal detector only picks up the iron. As a result the iron ends up hiding or "masking" the target. High-quality metal detectors are able to overcome this problem and detect targets even if they are right underneath the iron. The only other way to solve this problem is to make a rule to dig out whatever iron you detect if it's larger than, for example, 2 inches and check to see if there's anything else near it.

Nighthawking – The act of going metal detecting on private property without permission at night so you don't get caught. Also considered stealing, this is illegal and unethical.

Notching (Notch) – A form of discrimination, this is when you create a "rejection window" in the metallic spectrum so the detector ignores all metals that fall in that range. Another way of saying you stop a certain type of metal (or metals) from being detected.

Pinpointing – Determining the precise location of a target. Some metal detectors have a pinpoint feature that helps you find the target (using audio or visual clues) whereas some don't have this feature and you have to pinpoint manually. Both cases are discussed in the *"How to Hunt"* chapter.

Pinpointer – A small, handheld metal detector that's quite handy when you want to narrow down the exact location of the target. While a traditional metal detector finds the target area and tells you where to dig, a pinpointer helps determine where the treasure is within the hole. It's not absolutely vital to have, but it can seriously help you cut down on digging time.

Plug – One of the most commonly used terms in metal detecting. The plug is the area of soil/dirt you remove to find the target. When you've found the area where you need to dig, you shouldn't just shovel out the dirt in a random fashion. The right way of reaching your find is cutting out a plug which will go back into the soil once you're done with the hole. This is done by positioning your digger a couple of inches away from the target and digging around the target in a semi-circle. The blade should be slightly angled towards the target and you shouldn't dig a complete circle around the target. Instead, you should stop 80% of the way through and use the uncut part of the circle as a hinge. Using your digger you flip the plug out of the hole and locate your treasure. Once you're finished you put the round plug back into the hole and push it into place.

Power cable – The cable that connects the coil of the metal detector to the control box where the batteries are housed.

Pull tabs – These are the metal rings used to open aluminum cans and are a headache for metal detectorists for the same reason as *can slaw*.

Probe – A handheld tool that looks like a screwdriver and is used for finding coins.

Repeatable (signal) – Before you start digging you need to make sure the signal your detector picked up is repeatable. This means if you move it across the same area numerous times it will produce the same (or similar) signal. Real targets will produce repeatable signals whereas stray, non-repeatable signals indicate anomalies in the soil and that there's no need to dig.

Sensitivity- One of the most important settings on your metal detector. If you crank up the sensitivity your detector will be able to discover deeper targets but at the same time there is a higher probability of getting a false signal. Therefore, a perfect balance needs to be found so that your detector finds the targets but doesn't false.

Shaft – The frame of the metal detector which has the coil at the end, the control box higher up and the power cable connecting them. The shaft length is usually adjustable.

Sweeping/Swinging – The act of moving the metal detector across the ground in a side-to-side movement to detect metal.

Target ID – Many metal detectors have this feature which allows you to understand what's beneath your coil before you dig it up (not always correct).

Target Separation – High-end metal detectors are able to identify multiple targets that are in close proximity, which is known as target separation and can be quite helpful.

Threshold – Some metal detectors make a constant sound when being operated. This sound is known as the threshold and it changes when the coil passes over a target.

This is 99% of the vocabulary you will need to know in the field of metal detecting. There are dozens of other words for the many different types of coins or specific artifacts you may uncover but knowing those is not essential.

Index

Thank you

Thank you very much for reading this book. I

sincerely hope that you have enjoyed reading it and that you have found out plenty of useful and practical information. Metal Detecting is my passion and I am honoured to have shared my experience and knowledge with you.

If possible, please take the time to leave a review on Amazon.

I will be very grateful, and your review will help me enormously.

This is your chance to let other potential customers know about this book and how useful you found it.

Search for this book on Amazon –

"Metal Detecting: Treasure Hunting Bible for Beginners"

By Thomas Gold

Thank you so much for your time. Enjoy all your metal detecting adventures and finds.

Thomas Gold